すうじのおはなし

THE NUMBER STORY

SMALL BOOK ONE

ENGLISH - JAPANESE

---

*Numbers Teach Children
Their Number Names*

written and illustrated by

MISS ANNA

Early Reader Edition of *The Number Story 1*
Bronze Medal Winner, 2016 Wishing Shelf Book Award

Library of Congress Control Number: 2018902040

Names: Miss Anna, author.
Title: Number story : numbers teach children their number names / Miss Anna.
Description: Portland, OR: Lumpy Publishing, 2018.
Identifiers: ISBN 978-1-945977-13-8 | LCCN 2018902040
Summary: The pictures and rhymes present stories which introduce numbers 0-10.
Subjects: LCSH Numeration--English—Japanese--Pictorial works--Juvenile literature. | BISAC JUVENILE NONFICTION /
Languages: English--Japanese
Classification: LCC QA141.3 .M57 2018 | DDC 513—dc23

Publisher: Lumpy Publishing
Website: www.missannabooks.com
Email: missanna@missannabooks.com

Paperback: ISBN 978-1-945977-13-8
Printed in the U.S.A.   1 3 5 7 9 10 8 6 4 2

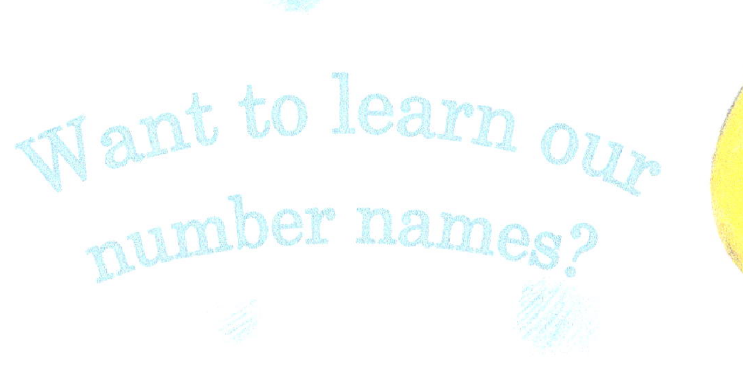

すうじのなまえをしってみたい？

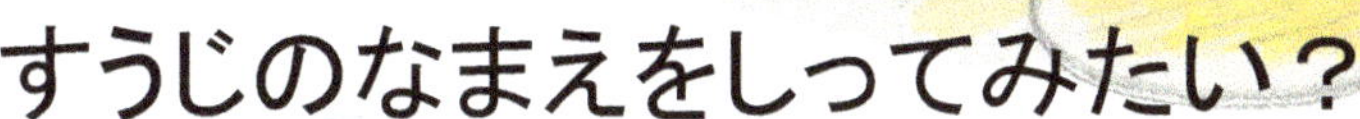

It is very easy and a lot of fun!

とってもかんたんでたのしいよ！

Say-along our little jingle

ぼくたちのおはなしをうたってみよう！

starting from Number One!

一ばんからはじめるよ！

1

ONE   looks like my one finger.

一はぼくのゆびみたい。

ONE!
一つ!

2

TWO   trails a tail.

二はおっぽがあるみたい。

A TAIL! おっぽ！

3

THREE   has bumps.

三はカーブをもってるよ。

BUMPY!　カーブをみて！

4

FOUR   carries a sail.

四はほをもってるよ。

4
A SAIL!
ヨット！

5
FIVE   is a racing track.
五はレーシングトラック。

VROOM!
1

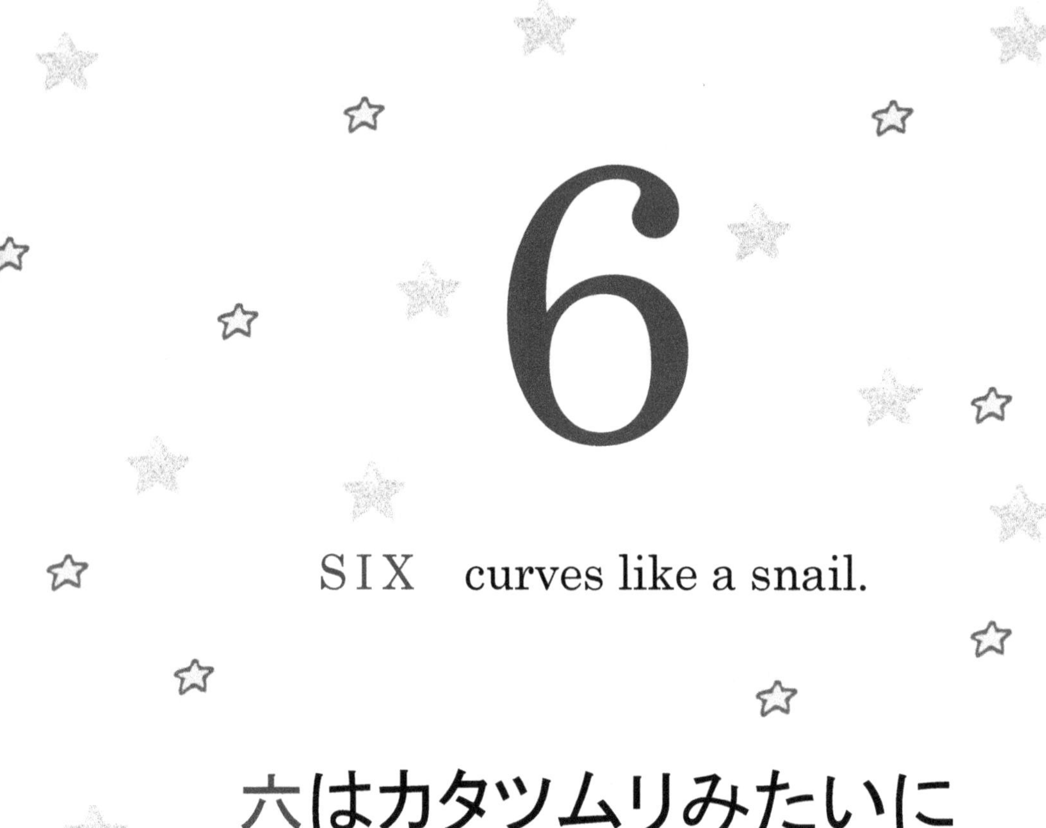

6

SIX   curves like a snail.

六はカタツムリみたいに
まがるよ。

A SNAIL!　カタツムリ！

7

SEVEN has a sharp angle.

七はするどいかくどを
もってるよ。

BE CAREFUL! IT'S SHARP!

とんがってるからきをつけて！

8

EIGHT   is rollercoaster rails.

八はジェットコースターだよ。

やったー！
YIPPEE!

NINE   is a bubble on a stick.

九はぼうのうえに
シャボンだまだよ。

A BUBBLE!　シャボンだま！

10

TEN is an eye of a whale.

十はくじらのめの一つだよ。

HELLO!　こんにちは！

And
そして
0
ZERO   is an empty pail.
ゼロはからっぽの
バケツだよ。

IT'S EMPTY!
からっぽ！

Thank you for playing with us today.

We had a lot of fun too!

きょうはぼくたちと
いっしょにうたってくれてありがとう。
とってもたのしかったよ！

We are your Number friends,
Zero to Ten,
Who will be here for you~

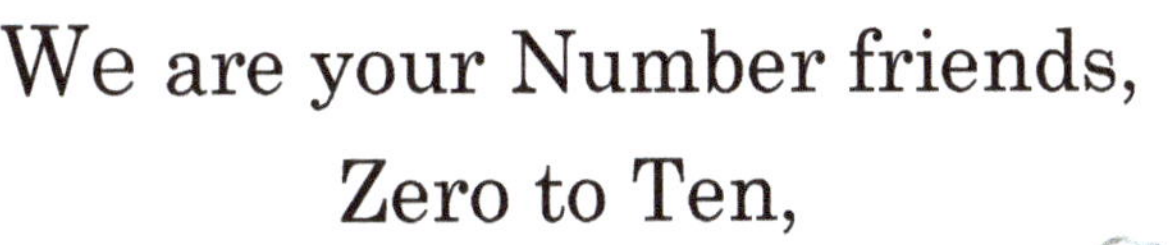

ぼくたちはきみのともだちだよ
ゼロから十。
いつもきみのそばにいるよ。

Bye-bye now!
See you again soon!

バイバーイ！
またあおうね！

The Numbers are *SINGING* too!

To sing-a-long, look for Miss Anna Number Story
at your favorite music store like iTUNES.

MP3

Numbers 0-10
IDENTIFYING
& COUNTING

Numbers 11-20
& Ordinals
first, second, third...

Numbers 0-100
& Place Values
ones, tens, hundreds...

About Clocks
& Telling Time
hours, minutes, seconds

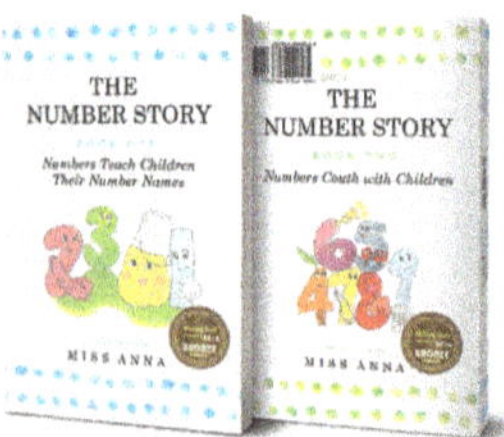

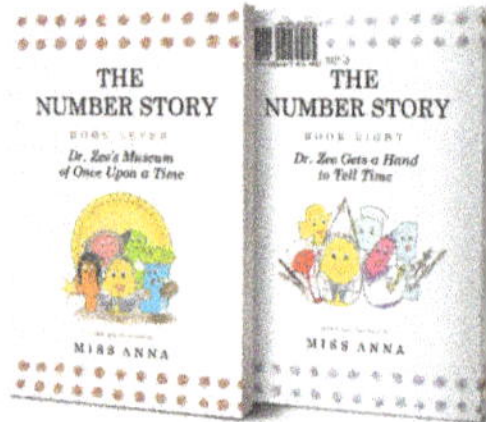

Number Story 1 & 2
isbn: 978-0-996216-48-7

Number Story 3 & 4
isbn: 978-1-945977-01-5

Number Story 5 & 6
isbn: 978-1-945977-06-0

Number Story 7 & 8
isbn: 978-1-949320-40-4

For more Miss Anna books to love,
visit us at

www.missannabooks.com

Numbers are working hard all over the world!
Come Travel the World with Us!

9 781945 977138